YOUR FATHER WALKS LIKE A CRAB

YOUR FATHER WALKS LIKE A CRAB

*Poetry For People
Who Hate Poetry*

Tolu' Akinyemi

STRANGE-IDEAS

'For in HIM *we live and move
and have our being.
As some of your own poets have said
we are* HIS *offspring.'*

Acts 17:28

All work herein by Tolu' Akinyemi except
And So It Ends Part I
by Somi Ekhasomhi

Cover design by Tolu Akinyemi
Photography by Femi Osewa

First published in Great Britain
by Heart of Words Publishing,
a trading name of
Strange Ideas (UK) Ltd. 2013

www.strangeideas.co
info@strangeideas.co

ISBN: 978-9789329199

www.poetolu.com
www.yourfatherwalkslikeacrab.com
www.instagram.com/poetolu
www.twitter.com/poetolu

CONTENTS

PREFACE

One cannot be certain if it is as despised as mathematics — or politics, but I know that many people, especially students, do not consider POETRY as one of their favourite things — a lot would go as far as declaring their 'hatred' for it.

Interestingly, many of such people enjoy reading, and appreciate other forms of literature, but readily link their apathy towards poetry to the humiliation and embarrassment they experience each time they struggle to relate or grasp depth from what is conventionally considered brilliant poetry. The obscure language — seemingly done intentionally — of such poetry and its subtle challenge to their intellectual capacity is a turn-off.

Quoting *W.H. Auden*, *"Most people enjoy the sight of their own handwriting as they enjoy the smell of their own farts"* and this very much applies to poets and their poems, and that uncertain air of subtly ambiguous grandiose they seem to effuse (especially critics who consider 'sentimental poetry' as inferior in artistry).

Even when they are not writing private poetry, in their intellectual exuberance and (slightly narcissistic) devotion to conformity with poetry principles, many poets forget to 'communicate'. They often end up with pedantic poetry that impresses some, intimidates some, but bores and fails to engage most.

I understand that there are different kinds of poetry, but it is undeniable that certain forms are considered 'superior' or 'the standard', their cryptic nature suggesting the dubious notion that poetry and its pleasures are for the intelligentsia.

There is a need for 'poetry without poets'. I am convinced that poetry, stripped of ego and pedantry, can be versatile enough to preserve its literary integrity and engage anyone who would not normally read or write poetry.

Poetry is an art, just like music, and if the ability to create music or even play a musical instrument is not a prerequisite for appreciating and enjoying good music, then the inability to write 'good poetry' or understand its intricacies must not deny anyone the pleasures of enjoying poetry.

Without any intention to ridicule complex forms of poetry, the poems in this book are written without the strictures of conformity and with a form and motive to portray poetry as enjoyable, especially to those people who would normally consider this literary form intimidating or boring.

I must also mention that this is not another collection of 'angry poetry'. Modern African poetry seems to increasingly reinforce the negative stereotypes of the Western World about Africa. They constantly reflect a lot of diatribe and angst in their portrayal of a rational African image of catastrophe and devastation, instability, poverty, war, economic and socio-political injustice.

A huge chunk of modern African literature is themed around this bias, so much that it appears difficult to be considered a serious African poet (or writer) if you do not write about these negative situations (and that, from a 'non-sentimental poetry' point of view). However, just as *Chimamanda Adichie* explains in *The Danger Of A Single Story*, these gloomy renderings reflect only a (negative) part of a bigger story, and a continual focus on it elevates the negative part to appear as the whole story, the only story.

As an African, who grew up in Africa, I know in despite of her challenges, Africans live in pursuit of happiness and laughter, we celebrate love and romance —comedians are rich, wedding ceremonies are big and lavish. We cherish fond memories of happy childhoods and growing up. We mourn when we lose loved ones and rejoice when a new life comes. We also enjoy the beauty of closely-knit families, the warmth of community and our wealth in social capital. Any African story that does not provide a balance on these perspectives is partial and incomplete.

With a fresh, whimsical and somewhat cheeky approach, *Your Father Walks Like A Crab* explores the dynamics of man's sentimental interactions and our ageless desire for mutual acceptance and affirmation. With a fair sprinkle of wit and humour, it is about relationships: familial, platonic or romantic; it is about beauty and of course, love – the love of it, the hate of it, the wait for it, the praise of it, the search for it, the find of it, the fall into it, the rejection of it and also the 'things' that get broken by it.

Your Father Walks Like A Crab also alludes to societal observations, moral and family issues within the panorama of African and religious values, while preserving an international relevance. Careful thought has been made by providing some insight into unfamiliar words or concepts that might interest a foreign reader.

I appreciate all my friends and admirers, especially from the social media, who inspired the desire to fulfil the agenda of this book. To every member of *Familia Poetica*, this would not have happened without you.

I feverishly hope each reader enjoys reading these poems as much as I relished writing them.

Tolu' Akinyemi

May 2013

ABOUT THE POET

Tolu' is a contracted form of *Toluwalope* which means 'God is worthy of praise'. *Akinyemi* means *A hero or warrior by fate*. Tolu' is a trained architect turned a writer. He was born in Akure, a sunny, sleepy Yoruba city in Western Nigeria. Some of his poems have appeared online and in printed anthologies such as *'Verses From The Sun'* (An Anthology of the Association of Nigeria Authors, Ondo, Nigeria).

His play *'The Big Society'* has been performed at the *Greenwich-Lewisham Young People's Theatre*, London, as part of a Stephen Lawrence Charitable Trust event.

'Your Father Walks Like A Crab' is his first published poetry collection.

ABOUT THE TITLE

I have been questioned about the title of this book and, besides the obvious reasons, here is an insight.

It was a few years ago, in the ancient town of *Akure*, Nigeria, where I was born. I sat in the passenger's seat of a car parked on a side street of a residential area, reading a book whose title I can't remember.

It was a very sunny day, not many people were on the street, but a lot were sitting or standing on the balconies and entrances of their homes. They were mostly having conversations or observing mundane activities on the street, while wooing cool air with hand fans, newspapers or kitchenware — I saw a young man fanning himself with the lid of a cooking pot.

There was the sound of approaching chatter just ahead of me, as four young men emerged from a street corner and walked towards the car in which I was seated. One of them had what I can only describe as a very dramatic disability.

As he hobbled towards me in the company of his friends, his legs made jerky, awkward bends, flying in all directions, as if fighting the wind. People on the street and in the shades were casting pitiful glances in his direction, while some really looked worried for him, cringing each time it seemed he would plunge sideways into the open roadside drainage. A few were staring rudely as well and, unlike his friends, they looked like they would be embarrassed to stroll alongside this young man who was *walking like a crab*.

I do not know where those silly words came from, but that was the way my mind instantly captioned his gait – anyone who has had a chance to observe them would agree that crabs indeed have a queer way of moving.

The jolly pack had surprisingly taken no cognizance of the fuss they had stirred; they were too carried away with their cheerful banter. Eventually, they reached and walked past me.

After I had taken a few guilty glances at the side mirror and concluded the phrase 'walks like a crab' would be an interesting title for a poem, something struck me: it doesn't matter how badly anyone or everyone else sees us, as long as we have the loyal covering of family and true friends who love us unconditionally, whether we walk like crabs, quack like ducks or chew like goats.

As I sat in that car, waiting for my friend who had stepped into a shop earlier, I remembered a saying in Pidgin English: *'monkey no fine, but him mama like am'*, which means 'the monkey is ugly, but his mother loves him'.

People considered as 'embarrassing' (whether inhumanly or deservedly) have faithful brothers, sisters, sons, daughters, parents and friends who are proud and protective of them. Even the most hated villains have people who love and adore them fiercely. True love is unconditional, unseasonal and sometimes irrational.

I realised that to find happiness, no one needs love from everyone; everyone only needs someone, and sometimes, that someone has to be you.

These thoughts and experiences inspired the title '*Your Father Walks Like A Crab*', which is also the title of a poem in this book.

1   To The Reader

I wonder
Has love found me
Or is this the wind?

2 THE POET AND THE POTTER

Poetry is (like) pottery
Words are (like) clay
Is the poet not (like) the potter?
In spawning surprises.

The potter surprises the clay
That never dreamt to be a pot
Now it imprisons a pond
The poet surprises words
With his mind, he makes them drunk
Till they speak in other tongues.

3   A NOTE OF WARNING

If you make me fall in love with you
Please don't say you were not warned
For as I fall, I'll break some bones
Lame in love to rise no more.

Start to count the cost
For it will take the world
To talk me out
Of making you my world.

Please don't leave your heart door ajar
Not even slightly, please be warned
For like a bandit, I will barge in
To build a wall across that door.

Get a court letter
But it will take forever
To pull me out
Of loving you forever.

Don't lead me on please I'm pleading
If you don't need a second skin
For like the dusk chases the dawn
I will, till our shadows become one.

Run with a thousand feet
Fly with a thousand wings
But I'll have to lose my sight
To lose you from my sight.

4 ## To The Girl
   ## Across The Street

Thursday evening, two minutes past six
You were standing by our street
With your (talkative) friend
Your skirt gently teasing the wind.

I overhead you saying you know me
(A neighbour from across the street)
So I assumed your (talkative) friend
With the funny-looking wig asked.

But more than her fake eyelashes
Your answer amused me
How could you say you know me?
When you don't feel the weight of my stare
Every morning as I run to my window
To swallow gulps of you
As you hurry off to work
Dressed in smiles and bright eyes.

If you know me, won't you notice?
How I collide my evening stroll
With your daily commute home
Just to struggle with the puzzle
Of how at the end of a busy day

You still look like it just began.

How could you say you know me?
When you don't even know it
How I strive to understand it
How easily you do it
To stand beside your (talkative) friend
And without even trying
You make her look so bad.

5 THE CHICKEN'S SOLILOQUY

I'm not deceived
They fatten me for the kill
Juicy pellets of millets
Golden grains of sweet corn
All for a cause.

I'm not deceived
They protect me till a feast
A royal coop from fresh *bamboo*
They drive the snakes faraway
Of course for a cause.

I'm not deceived
I'm alive to be skinned
I've seen cousins at dawn
Ushered out to see the world
But at dusk, their cages lie empty
Telling a buffeting tale.

6 THE DILEMMA OF OLUFUNMI

Olufunmi the beauty queen
Olufunmi, fair as the hibiscus
Eyes of gems like morning dew
The village men bowed at her feet.

Farmers, teachers
Traders, the village doctor
Carpenters, the village beggar
Everyone wanted her as a bride.

The farmer came, hoe across torso
Cutlass in his hand, smelling of herbs
And *Olufunmi,* had her three requests
Will I have a car, a sports car to drive?
Do you own a house, one with marble floors?
Do you have cash, to squander around?

Herbiodun smiled and then shook his head
My bike has a carriage — you'll ride at my back
My hut door is low — please walk in head bent
And I have a clay safe — a coinful of it.

But Olufunmi had heard enough
Seething and hissing, she threw herbman out.

The teacher came, shirt starched into steel
Double-bent with books he brought to impress
Olufunmi's questions remained the same
I will need a car to flaunt all around
Do you have a house, with chandelier lights?
How fat is your bank, *bamboo* or *baobab*?

Bookola grunted, adjusted his tie
Fair like your eyes is my motor bike
I bought bricks and beams, soon I'll buy the land
The money? Don't worry, my pension is fat.

By now Olufunmi was pacing the room
And soon 'steel collar' was chased with a broom.

Then came chief *Oleku*, the rich contractor
With breezing *agbada* and an entourage
But *Olufunmi* won't sway easily
I love convertibles, will you get for me?
Does 'house with a garden' describe where you live?
And rooms filled with money from different
countries?

Then Chief *Oleku* — beamed with a smile
A convertible — each day of the week?
Houses with gardens — views of the sea?
A bed decked with money — tell me what you think?

These words were barely out of his mouth
When dazed Olufunmi went down in a swoon

But twenty-one buckets of water later
Their honeymoon plans were already made.

The honeymoon ended, her sun became sore
She learnt Chief *Oleku* has a family
Four beautiful daughters and two growing sons
From four wives who were also tricked to the moon.

olufunmi* agbada* bamboo* baobab* oleku *

7   My Wife Is Mad At Me

What *wahala* is this?
My wife is mad at me
And won't tell me why.

She had gone in
Came out, all dressed
In a lovely yellow dress
I bought few years ago
On a trip to Tobago.

It was a perfect fit
Now it seems small
Two sizes or more
(So I mentioned it).

What *wahala* is this?
She's still mad at me
I still don't know why.

wahala*

8 WITH NO CHAPERON

If I could have no care at all
Save to frown, the sun woke me
That freedom, if I could have
Of a child with no chaperon
Free to roam till dusk beckons
Or as free as a bachelor
At liberty to fart all night
Or why not? He sleeps alone.

9   GO HIDE YOUR HUSBAND

I know you remember
Why he married you
You had this attire
The size of a scarf
The hems didn't gather
And he loved it too.

So go hide your husband
I have to warn you
And should you do wonder
The cause of alarm
Some girls crossed the border
A scarf all they wear.

10   Taken Every Time

On a mango tree
That lives by the roadside
I never find a ripe fruit.

On a pathway
That leads to the market place
I never find a gold ring.

Yet fruits get ripe
On the road side tree.

And gold is lost
On the market pathway.

But like good women
Another finds before me.

11 UJU

Beauty-ful *Uju*
I need to hide
Your eyes pierce me
Like sweet *juju*.

Wow-thou-ful *Uju*
Where do I hide?
Your smiles pull me
Like hot *fufu*.

uju* fufu* juju*

12 YOUR FATHER WALKS LIKE A CRAB

(Rich boy to poor boy)
Your father walks like a crab
His oily mouth needs a swab
Your father has just two clothes
A brown worn robe, a dirty grey coat.

(Poor boy to rich boy)
Yes, my father walks like a crab
Yes, he is an old smelly farmer
But a fiercely loving father
Who cares like a mother.

(Poor boy's friend to rich boy)
Your father walks like a panther
He wears gold, silk and leather
But you share him with ten brothers
From ten a-whoring mothers.

13   AND SO IT ENDS PART I

I cry, shout
I ask you to leave
And never come back
The door slams
Behind you
As you go
Is this the end?

Right now
I don't care
I watch
As you walk away
You don't look back
Not even once.

I wait
For a call
Or a text
A message
On my wall
Another apology
I can furiously reject
But you don't try
You don't call.
You don't stand by my window
Waiting for a glimpse of me

You don't wait outside my door
Hoping to talk to me
You don't haunt my favourite spots
Hoping to run into me
You don't call my friends
Asking them to help you
Make me love you again
The things you don't do
Are much more painful
Than what you have done
Before.

I am still angry
If you came around
I'd slam the door
In your face
But how I long
For you to come around
So I wait
Till waiting turns to longing
And to sadness
I wait, and wait
But you're done
You're done
With "I'm sorry"
With proving how much
You do love me
In fact it seems
You're done with me.

14 And So It Ends PART II

You cried
I was calm
But cried in my heart
You asked me to leave
I did leave
The door
Slammed
In my face
Like a gunshot
In my brains.

I did leave
My head held high
But my heart crushed down
I walked
Away.

I hoped you'll call me back
Though with assails
(To save your pride)
You didn't
(So I saved mine)
And walked away
Feeling the holes
Your eyes bored in my back
As you peered from behind

The window blinds
Already baptised
In your tears.

You did not call me back
As each step I took
Took me
Away from you.

Like grains in the mouth
Of a ten-day old child
I choked
As lumps formed in my throat
My heart
Turned back
But my pride
Held me back
Twice a day
At dawn and its dusking tail
I'd dial your phone
But my pride
Always won.

I have confessions —
Unsent, SMS, e-mails
All unsent
The backspace
Always won.
But now

My heart
Has lost its hue
And my days
Are in grayscale
Now I know
Folly is a man
That bears my name.

What guns won't
What wars won't
Pride would
Take from a man
I might not do all
To get what I want
But I should
Have done all
To keep what I got.

To my ego
I lost
The only pearl
I ever found —
Can ever find
That day I walked away
When I reasoned
With my feet.
But now
I'm coming
Back

To the only home
I've always known
I only hope
You still stand
By that door
That once slammed
In my face
Shutting daylight
From my day.

I hope
You still wait
Though with venom
On your lips
But with love
In your limbs
That when
I've humbly bathed
In the rain of your wrath
I eventually get squashed
In a long-felt embrace.

Yes, I'm done
With saying I'm sorry
Now
I'll stay sorry.

Yes, I'm done
With saying how much

I do love you
Now I'll prove
To love you is all,
The only thing I can do.

And so it ends
Our loving forth and back
Like a twig in the tides.

And so it ends
Door slamming
And reasoning with my legs.

And so it all ends
For this is the last time
I'll need to say
I'm sorry.

15 TO THE MEN

To the men who lie to women
To the men who ogle women
To the men who cheat women
To the men who cheat on women
To the men whose panacea is "I'm sorry"
To the men who hide their wedding rings
To the men who hunt women
To the men who 'bought' their wives
To the men who chase schoolgirls
To the men who think with their manhood
To the men who take pride in their 'conquests'
To the men who don't improve
To the men who travel with 'blankets'
To the men who can never say "No!"
To the men who are uncommitted to commitments
To the men who trivialise things
To the men who cannot just be friends
To the men who visit at odd hours
To the men who are vulgar
To the men who will start living responsibly when
married
To the men who don't call back
To the men who bore you with calls
To the men who don't show public affection
To the men who just don't care
To the men who can't recognise limits

To the men who can recognise limits but can't keep to
limits
To the men who buy you lunch and want you for
dinner
To the men who disrespect women
To the men who stretch the truth
To the men who are overly friendly (with your
friends)
To the men who give strangers 'a ride'
To the men who cannot cook
To the men who can cook, but would never cook
To the men who can brag and so they brag
To the men who are not handy with things
To the men who never played chess
To the men who always ask for help
To the men who never ask for help
To the men who are opportunists
To the men who act funny when you act nice
To the men who don't know when they can't win
To the men who don't know when they just lost
To the men who hide their phones
To the men who are handsome and cocky
To the men who won't allow you tidy their bedrooms
To the men who fall in love several times
To the men who will know tomorrow only what they
know today
To the men who don't buy books
To the men who buy books and don't read them
To the men who can't play any musical instrument

To the men whose soccer games come first
To the men who must taste 'the pudding' and then
say "I do"
To the men who don't want to get married
To the men who doubt this poet is a man
To the men I don't want to be.

16 MAD THREADS

Said the dove to the owl
Human beings!
Could their threads be mad?
It's hard to explain
Why more upon more
Their clothes misbehave
Could their threads be mad?

Said the owl to the dove
Human beings!
Their threads must be mad
What else would explain?
Why clothes hate to stay
On their women's skin
Their threads must be mad.

17 THE WOMAN IS DEAD

The Woman is dead
Yet nobody cries
Reckless 'sexy' things
Usurped her instead.

The Woman is dead
And nobody cares
Town-painting 'hotties'
Have taken her stead.

18   UNSPOKEN WORDS

Unspoken words
Roaring louder than the stomps
Of Alexander's troops
Levelling the streets of Greece
Multiples of unspoken words
Birthed from a spoken word
Or a lingering gaze
Or mere shadows of a sigh.

Your lips are sealed
But in deafening amplitudes
Your dressing speaks
You've probably said one word
But I surely heard ten more
Un-opaquing that smile
Revealing your grime
Now I know what you are.

19 PEOPLE OF THE NIGHT

People of the Night
I doff my hat
Making ends meet
By dimming the lights
In between the sheets
Distilling a kill.

People of the night
A pat for your back
Making ends meet
Harassing the night
Honest eyes have found sleep
Yours prowl the streets.

People of the night
Be on your guard
Whatever you want
You always get
But nemesis too
Is easy to find.

20   Twenty Children

Twenty Children
Will not be playmates
For twenty years
They become workmates
Secretly intimidated
By each (climbing) step
The others make
Till they all run
(Here and there)
Inspired by fear.

21 # THE WANDERING MAN

You
Keep leaving
(This back door open)
But your children
And wife
Patiently wait
Perhaps one day

                                    You
                        Will
                Come
        Back
Home
To put a wall
Across that door.

22 STOLEN WATER AND THE HOUSE OF SLAUGHTER

The night had sent the sun to sleep
And yet he took a stroll at ease
Upon a path the wise desist
And there she lives, with honeyed lips
Clad in strips she laid in wait
And for a prey to pass her way.

And soon he passed that lonely street
That certain path the wise desist
She caught his hand and drew him near
To nibble gently on his ear
Her eyes, they speak a thousand dreams
Her voice will lure a troop to sleep.

My husband is away she said
Not very soon will he return
I drowned my bed in lavish scents
Perfumes of hyacinth and myrrh
And so come in and have no fear
Feed on my flesh without a care.

He knew he was a lucky one
Just like the fools who came before
Into her house the home of death
Unto her bed the road to hell

He did not know it like the fish
Which fancied a bait as a meal.

Knew not his life hung on a hair
Until her claws tore through his heart
And then he fell without a fight
And then she rose without ado
To toss his bones upon the heap
Of previous fools she made a meal.

Her face she patted with some talc
Her bosom, into place she heaved
She stepped again into the streets
And suddenly she wore a smile
Because she heard approaching feet
Another fool will soon be food.

23   FRUIT FOR THOUGHT

I have blistered my lips
Entreating reason
But to anyone or me
You will not listen.

This fruit is rotten
You swear it ripens
But soon these flies
Will open your eyes.

24 A NIGHT BY THE NIGER BANK

Under the sky
That makes the Niger drunk
Under the clouds
That inebriates her
With an offering of rain
Under the sky
Have I found my rest
On a bed of sand.

Fireflies like chandeliers
A living roof above my head
Slumber wears me like a cloak
My heart beating in rhythm
To a classical orchestra
Of croaking frogs
As I carefreely await
The vicissitudes of dawn.

25   AN AFRICAN NIGHT

Night time is here
Honest men are inside
Seated by fire
Telling tales of tortoise's escapades
To sparkling eyes and listening ears
Of wife and children around the flames
They laugh and dance
Wielding spits of roasted meat
Eerie light from the lamp of flames
Playing hide and seek on their faces.

Silhouettes that once were trees
Lost in the gloom of the sombre dusk
Huddled by the wind
Rustling in whispers
In the language of the night
The trees make faces
Funny scary leafy faces
Diurnals and nocturnals exchange greetings
On their way to and from home.

Owls rehearse their sombre tunes
Sages stare into the night
Pretending to understand
The moon fights back the sleep
Besieged with a shore of stars

Like several tiny gnats
In the dark and silent sky.

Pregnant women hide indoors
Scared to tread the lurking night
Lest demons suck their babies
Tired potbellied children
Scamper behind their mothers
They do not want to lean on walls
Lest demons seep in with a slop.

26 MIDNIGHT

The day's first hour
And my mind starts
A riot
That stinks
            of silence!

Like rumours of war
On a crowded market square
My thoughts run amok
Still
        Silence!

27 Falling Out

For me the days are falling
Out of the basket
While other people gather days
In more baskets
It is scary that one day
Because I have run out of days
This basket would lie empty
And I would need to give it
To someone who would put it to a better use.

I look up to see everyone around me
Looking forward to tomorrow
While I look away
As I already know what to expect.

The days are falling out of this basket
Ad when it is empty
I will have no choice
But to lay it down
This is a plea to whoever finds it —
Please put it to a better use.

28   A RIVED MIND

Blessed by the souls I've met
So far in this odyssey
Blessed by great moments shared
Cursed I had to say goodbye.

Discomfort is bursting forth
Milling my heart to a pulp
Choking me with emotions.

Twenty playmates will not play
Together for twenty years
I separated from nineteen playmates
I'm cursed by nineteen playmates
Because each one departed
With a chunk of my heart.

29 A PAIN OF TWO SIDES

Stop telling me
You feel my pain
Yours is
From too much to eat
Mine is
From nothing to eat.

30 ILLUSIONS

High castles on fluffy clouds
Swift cruises on lofty winds
Merry swims in cooling streams
Lazy lolls by lushly springs
The flawless dwelling of acute chumps
The precipitous zenith of fatuity
The abysmal bowel of utopian thirsts
The speedy peaking of nirvanic bliss
Sweet, swift yet ephemeral, brief
Lovely, heavenly yet transient, thin
Loungy loafs on royal thrones
Princely treats at bounteous feasts
Lavish trips and shopping sprees
Hefty wealth of unearthly means
Wads in stacks in bags and sacks
And then a quick and hasty grab
Brings reality staring back
Then laments of the fool begin
About the crisp notes in his dream.

31 To Please The *Oga* At The Top

It's like shaking a tree
Shaking the trunk
Of a *baobab* tree.

It's like whistling a tune
Whistling a tune
And trying to smile.

It's like having a bath
Having a bath
And staying dry.

oga*

32   SPRINKLES IN BETWEEN

It won't always, end with a kiss
Hearty cheers or gleaming bliss
Happy songs often will die
Beaming smiles will fall asleep
Merry laughter tumbles ill
Some life's sprinkles in between.

33   To Find The Perfect Bride

Here on earth far, far away
Behind a wall of lovely hills
Lives a town of women pure
Blameless in all perfection
Chaste in beauty and in deeds.

They all seek a common goal
To find a man to make their own
But with very curious terms
Like a three-prong fork, three in all
Meet them all, you'll have a bride.

Such a man must be a man
Who has never told a lie
Such a man must be a man
Who has never touched the rain
Such a man must be a man
Who has never tasted grains.

34 THE EX -IT

He sat on the right
A smirk on his smile
She sat on the left
Her latte on her eyes
They ne'r said a word
She drained her latte.

As she left on the right
She niftily pushed
A note in his hand
His smile on a smirk
He knew the note said
"I miss you so much".

A smirk on his smile
He opened and read
And all the note said
Had just two words more —
"Get over it, I got over you".

35 THE NEXT RUNG

Everyone needs a friend
We were great friends
And all was well.

We talked of politics and social ills
That is what friends talk about
And all was well.

But the day you raised your foot
For a hold on the next rung
All ceased being well.

36   A POEM-MAKING EPISODE

Time took a break and sat by me
On lush grass banking a gentle stream
Euphonies escaped my breath
Like psychedelic butterflies
As I made love to a poem.

I gave birth to woven words
From the loom of my heart
The wind ricocheting its allure
Like raindrops on tropical rocks.

Hypnotized, time sat by me
Inebriated willingly
By the libation of my lips
Envious streams flowed by in bliss
Witnessing our union, my poem and me.

37 THE POEM I NEVER WROTE

Concealed, unheard, unseen
Yearning direly to be free
From the nib of my pen, to be spilled.

I broke you into words
Whose worth would mock the seas
Filled with precious stones abrim.

Into words
Whose worth derides the pride
of any king or queen who is, or did ever exist.

I imagined you a poem
And chained it in my head
(A poem of) you, amok in my head.

(A poem of) you
Robed with words, beyond words
Words so pretty, yet to exist.

Words that plead
For freedom fervidly
Impatient to gape
At whom they describe so intensely
Words, of bits of you, your hips or even your lips.
Or your eyes!

Your eyes!
Your eyes in words
Your eyes!
In words
Your eyes in words
Now
Thoughts of those crystal balls
Slowly lull me to a dream.

(A dream of) words
As threads in a poem
Of you amok in my head
Unwritten, un-breathed
Never to be heard, or read
By you, not even me
Or anyone who is, or is yet to exist.

38 THE TREASURE BOX

Someone fetch a long ladder please
You do not deserve to be in a treasure box
Why would anyone put a treasure in a box?
Is it not like plucking a star from the sky?
A limiting shelter to bestow on it
When the sky — the only roof she needs.

You do not deserve to be in a treasure box
I did not find you to hide you in a treasure box
I do not even like the sound of 'a treasure box'
A treasure in it or not, a box is a box
So call it what it is — a cage, a prison
You do not deserve to be in a box.

I'll sprint the streets with flashing teeth
A child announcing his new toy
Making his friends, with envy green
Please where is that long ladder?
And where is the tallest roof?
I will announce you to the world.

39 One Sempiternal Episode

Keepsakes keep gentle memories un-stale
Miles away, I found a friend
Insight impinges hindsight
Grasping firm a truth confirmed —
Events, people, are merchants of purpose.

40 A Sea Of Dreams

A sea of dreams
Impinge with the fury of the wind
When hapless blades of elephant grass sway
For mercy, to be spared in its path.

A sea of dreams
Like the news of war
On a crowded street
Rampaging like a mob of mad cows.

A sea of dreams
A mouth that speaks from a box of light
Faraway, an ocean of ears listen
Bewitched by the light.

A sea of dreams
Pressed into the faces of books
Read like a treasure
By the eyes of an ocean of ears.

A sea of dreams
Of mere thoughts that earned life
Hills of coalesced steel and glass
Works of a dreamer's mind.

A sea of dreams
Strengthened and weakened with time
But with the heart of a slave
Drinking from the brinks of escape.

Like the sea, dreams might quieten
But they don't sleep
With time, a stream will seep home
Even from a prison of glass.

41 THE SIREN'S CALL

A thousand priests
Could have said it
A thousand times
I'll disbelieve (that)
This encounter
Is not a dream.

For across myriad miles
Niftily through phone lines
I heard a siren's voice
Yet, I'm alive.

42 DON'T SAY WITH YOUR EYES ONLY

Beneath a tree of hollies
Alone my love and me
I coo in words you only
Will ever hear from me.

Your eyes they tell a story
Love of the purest breed
They speak in allegories
Each time you stare at me.

Like honey to the belly
Are words of love spoken
Don't say with your eyes only
The love you have for me.

43 # AGAIN
(A POEM FOR A DAY TO VALENTINE'S DAY)

Rumbling thumps
Of approaching drums
Dancing feet outside my walls
Louder!
With each day's trudge
Nearer!
With each clock tock
Previously mere signs of sound
Arriving-ly turning to sight
Then yearly reality bites.

Dancing feet outside my walls
Drunk with odes of folks in love
But in this room
The hush is harsh
Silence!
Silence loudly shouting out
Again the fourteenth day arrives
Again your gift is pretty, wrapped
Pretty, wrapped, but still untagged.

44 THE GRAVEYARD BENCH
(ANOTHER POEM FOR A DAY TO VALENTINE'S DAY)

A faraway look, her palms on knees
Among permanent stone-cold beds
For men whose life snore permanently
Like the sombre bench at the graveyard
That grieving people seat upon.

The eve of another fourteenth of the second
Her bench still lounges amongst the graves
Silent, except for the rustling leaves
Seated alone, surrounded by planted stones
Lullabies from lonely winds sullenly blowing.

She wants it in a lively garden
Seated on it with a living man
Exchanging smiles and holding hands
But she is stuck on this graveyard bench
In the company of men turned meals to worms.

Who knows what miracle is at hand?
Tomorrow might herald her smiles
Swapping this for a bench in the park
A rainbow in the sky and a roof of butterflies
What miracle is at hand, who knows?

45 TO COOK A STONE

Don't ask me
How I feel
A butcher doesn't flinch
When he leads the humble sheep
The way the stew is cooked.

Don't pull me
From my tears
That drown me every day
By words you always say
And ones you never say.

Don't tell me
I'll be fine
When you know in your mind
You had the cure I need
But gave it all to him.

Don't mock me
With your smiles
At me, it holds no warmth
I've seen you smile at dusk
And turn the night to dawn
Because you smiled at him.

I'm lost
So forlorn
But hope made my heart home
Time, eventually
Will turn a hill to dust.

46 A CARAMEL CANDY POT

If a pot of caramel candy was a woman
In her eyes would be a secret-laden twinkle
Twinkling innocent eyes you can't decipher
Her rubik's cube-smile would make you smile
Then lure you till you're lost
She would be good to your eyes
And be bad for your heart
But your pulsing puzzled mind
Would barely put up a fight
Yet after the fight is lost
She'll still nurse you to your cure.

If a pot of caramel candy was a woman
She would have tender story-teller lips
That host winking scented trails
In shades varying to and back
From rainbow hues to gothic black
She would have two subtle dimples
On tomato cheeks that scream cuddle me.

If a pot of caramel candy was a woman
She would stand beside another
She is head and shoulder taller than
The other could really lean forward
And still would not be found.

47 IF I FALL IN LOVE

If I fall in love
The sun will still rise at dawn
And take a break at dusk.

If I fall in love
Politicians will still lie
And folks would never learn.

If I fall in love
Peace might still elude the Middle East
We might find Bin Laden lives.

If I fall in love
A lot could change, or remain the same
But why should I care?

Everything ceased to exist
Everyone became extinct
That day love found us.

A new world was made
With only you, then me
Then nothing else mattered anymore.

48 VALERIE

Like you promised me, Valerie
Would you still come over?
Do you recall — it's bus forty-four?
Three stops from Sainsbury's.

I'll still cook you dinner, Valerie
Like I bragged yesterday
I'm boiling water already
For amala with gbegiri.

I'll eat and watch you eat, Valerie
Your hand buried in gbegiri
Could there be a ring in it?
Would I ask you to marry me?

amala* gbegiri*

49 # THE BULLY
(FOR DOLAPO)

The glow in her eyes
Daily bully the sun
Weary and beaten
It gives up each dusk.

I laughed at the sun
So silly you are
God made you first (but)
Saved t'best for her eyes.

dolapo*

50 # CLUMSY SANDALS ARE NOW SHOES
(FOR TOSIN)

"Sir-rrrrrr!" he would ring
With a voice whistle-shrill
He would answer his name
From a curious house corner.

He would hobble scurrying out
Struggling under a backpack
Now the cat meows with a roar
And clumsy sandals are now shoes.

tosin*

51   MINDING AYOMIDE

I do not understand
This queer behaviour
Of Mama *Ayomide*
It was her idea, not mine
That I keep a watchful eye
On her rascally son
She said I could even spank him
Should there be a need
Now she wants my other eye
She says I raised my voice
Too loudly at her child.

ayomide*

52   MY PAINTED LADY

Gleefully skipping
Over the broad green lilies
Her course keeps winding
Unsure like the wind.

Each moment I'm certain
She wills for a landing
Each moment I'm wrong
Till I see her no more.

painted lady*

53   SAWUBONA

Firm roots sourcing from one stout trunk
Tentacles spreading from one same source.

I hear you my brother
Deep calling to the deep
My heart calls back, to your heart's cry out
I hear you my brother
Like a cub and the mother's outcry
Over the hills that lead to the lair.

I see you my brother
The evidence of my identity
Seeing myself with my own eyes
I see you my brother
Like twin seeds from the pods of a nut
They call me me, because you exist.

I feel you my brother
As real as you can be
Beyond the air that I breathe
I feel you my brother
Like the heat upon my skin
Or the soil beneath my feet.

I know you my brother
One vein coursed by one blood

Two bodies enclosing one mind
I know you my brother
Your length, breadth and width
Words you'll say, and out about to breathe.

sawubona*

54 THE SHADE

Gathering clouds across the sky
I sit smiling, you on my mind
Chunks of hail, about to rain
All over my heart
The sun shines away.

Red up high, the sun burns bright
I feel peace with the look in your eyes
My skin, the sun swears to sear
But my heart stays cool
'Neath the shade of your eyes.

55 YOU

You make me
Calm like the hills
Sometimes
Rough like the seas.

You give me
Joy like a stream
Sometimes
A harvest of sighs.

You take me
To the peak of the hills
Sometimes
To the pith of the pits.

You show me
Love like a god
Sometimes
Hurt like a sword.

When you're gone
I'm at war
And I'm at peace
When you're long.

When you're here
I'm at peace
And I'm at war
When you're near.

56 MY DAME'S GAME

I met a dame
A pretty dame
I asked her name
She purred away
My name?
Not today.

I met the dame
Another day
I asked again
She purred the same
My name?
Not today.

I know my dame
Must have a name
And so I'll wait
Till when she'll say
My name?
Yea today.

57 MAMIHLAPINATAPAI

This silence —
This silence is sound
It's seashore sand
Resisting the waves
It's angry flames
Fighting the rain
But smiles can't disguise
The look in your eyes.

mamihlapinatapai*

58 QUANDARY

Don't scream if I slip
Through your iffy grip
You close your door
And say welcome.

I do not know
What not to believe
Your lips say please
But your eyes can kill.

To flee from your gaze
Or cling to your words
Is to stand between bulls
And a flaming pit.

59   COM-PROMISED

"I promise you —"
How many times
Have you heard those words?
And all the colourful ones
That attend them
Hanging like innocent halos
But dropping eventually
Like rotten mangoes
Few drop around your feet
Many squarely in your face
Filling your ears with rotten juice
Now words no longer excite you.

60   THEN TIME HAPPENS

Memories sublime into time
Memories entrust its beauty with time
But with time, time erodes the splendour
Diluting sweet memories in the mind
A day at a time.

True goodbyes are those words
You choke on in tears
Then time that lazy artist
Repaints it all with hazy lines
Blurring memories away
Like bile spilled on a lovely meal.

Still on time, the greedy sage
Bullying us all with his old age
He never forgets, yet never shares
The silent thief that steals all things
With an unspoken warning and a tick.

61   TIME

Like a whiff of smoke
From a burning stove
Like words out spilled
That can't be retrieved
Some watch it tick
Some run with it
Some are in its scripts
Some observe the scene.

62 Heaven Seems Far Away

Sometimes all I want to do
Is run inside and hide
Behind the veils of music
Or beneath bed sheets
In a deathlike solace sleep.

Sometimes all I want to do
Is open my mouth and scream
Loudly at my uncertainties
Please simply let me be
Let me be what He wills.

I know all I need to do
Is close my eyes on my knees
My dried out mouth is wide
But soulless words saunter out
And heaven seems far away.

63   A SINISTER GREETING

Like they always say
'A happy birthday to you'
As days creep up on you
A year at a time
You gladly make merry
While a carnivore stalks the prey
Edging you up that path
Man's footsteps die out.

64 THOUGHTSICLES

Dreamy eyes often see no sleep
Aching hearts hide behind skin
A thousand unneeded wants
Will not quieten a true need.

From the mouth of a crazy mind
The truth will sometimes saunter out
As 'senseless' is merely a little sense less
So dissect all things with a heart that seeks.

65   SLOW DOWN

I close my eyes as I write
Looking into the eyes of time.

He stares back
I can't see a thing
Or rather those things
I deeply wish to see.

Those memories I lounged through
Growing up and childhood
Friends I had and once knew
Now thrown around the globe
Splintered into places I do not know.

Why do we meet and part?
Why do we have to say goodbye?
(The few times we even have the chance)

I feel like a reunion
Meeting everyone I've ever known
In one huge hall
All over again
I can't stop thinking
Of how sweet it will be
But can that ever be?
It is hard, but it is true

I've met people
I'll never meet again
Till that moment I'll follow
That path of shadows.

They will be alive somewhere
Occasionally remembering me (or maybe not)
But nothing can be done about it.

We might live in the same city
We might even have a narrow brush
Maybe come a mile near each other
But it just won't happen.

I feel like a time capsule
Standing before a wide wall
With my life's sweet memories
Displayed upon it.

I've said it before
Once more won't hurt
When old memories
Are taken from a man
What is the essence of his life?

So I have learnt
To briefly silence time
Regurgitating special moments of each day
The things I did, people I did meet.

I've said it before
Once more won't hurt.

The journey is not always
About its end
Sometimes the thrill is in the ride

Time!
Seasons!
Changes!
Living!
Life!
Places!
Faces!
Ageing!

Slow down
People slow down
Take time
Slow down
Today won't always be
And while it is, remember it

I've said it once
Once more won't hurt.
Don't live life in haste
Catch memories of each day
You'll surely need them someday.

Don't rush through your life
To the other side of your years
Naked of the memories
Of how you got there.

66   A SUMMARY

Days pass away
Stolen by the tick of time
Memories all gone.

–

Like rain kissing earth
I met people in my life
To meet no more.

–

Roses everywhere
I stretch out to have a hold
Taken every time.

–

Filled to the brim
As a fast flowing stream
No tributaries.

67 THE WANTED

She used to think it sweet
Each time a man says
"I am in love with you"
Now she knows
It never will be sweet
Till she's the one saying it.

68 JASMINA

Seas of silver
And hills of gold
I have none of both
But what Leonardo's oil
Did Mona Lisa
This Poet's ink
Will do you Jasmina
With words
The ones unborn
Will not believe
So till we see
Keep saving the world
With your Mediterranean smile.

69 SHIRK-ETARIES

Oaken barriers to the hall of help
Imperial lords, heart glazed with rocks
With stone-cold face
Bedizened with dubious smiles.

With thick lip-sticked lips
And shadowed eyelids?
Or modest 'deeper-lifed' face?
They are all the same.

With laser glances
Tearing a hole in your ego
Every rap on her desk is
By preset from those pests —
Job applicants!
Favour seekers!

Sang-froid frying shirk-etaries
You will not reach the hall of help
As long as she sits in between
Not with that look
Gauging the age of your shoes.

She knows that cheap perfume
She definitely sees that suit
Hanging on you

Like the pouch of a kangaroo
And that rag you call a tie
Strangling you at the neck.

The director is always in a meeting
And don't bother to leave a note
You'll be leaving fodder for the bin.

70 THE NAG

Her words, like rain
Like salty rain
With poison for honey
Bile for a meal
With fangs for fury
Venom for lips.

71 THE OBSERVER

I've heard many songs
Great songs, croaks of frogs
Some think they can sing
But spout prickly heat.

I've watched people sleep
Whisperers in their dreams
With baritone snores
You'll swear it's a horn.

72 THE MIRACLE

It's a week since my dear wife last talked to me
She would hear me, but not say a word
I would talk; she would stare and not respond
She has won by miles this silence war.

It's an hour since *Iya Bose*
Brought money owed my wife
Like a good husband, I took it to her
Then a miracle happened—

My wife who has been deaf for a week
Heard me — and even spoke to me
With a deafening scream and fiery eyes
When I asked to hold the money a while—
A deposit for my new Toyota.

iya bose*

73   When The Music Stops

Restless feet twitch in unease
Awaiting the pace-setter beat
From the agile *dundun* drummer.

He heaves his massive drum up his shoulder
Drawing the leathery strap
Nearer his fattened neck
As the brass bells respond
With a ting-a-ling
The twitch of restless feet
Turns into tense rhythmic thuds
On the soft rain-soaked soil.

Then like a host of rain hammers
With a clatter, pounding on zinc roofs
The drums roll like sheets of thunder
Working a frenzy, into the possessed dancers.

They twirl and swirl
Animated with reckless abandon
Throwing jocund limbs up
In every direction
About in jaunty random.

Ayanyemi's hands work like a heedless rotor
His eyes beaming with a sparkling fire

As the dancers respond to the slaps
On the flattened leathery faces.

The drummers stare at each other
Ayanyemi and *Ayanwale* stare at each other
Like menacing rival wrestlers
Skilfully flaunting rhythmic prowess
Taunting tauted hide, with slender sticks.

The human spindles threaten to burst
The euphony like a fever working on them
They dance and dance
And dance and dance
Smacking their lips
To the symphonic delicacy.

Ayanyemi and *Ayanwale* kept swimming
They kept swimming in a pool of sweat
As with a climaxing rat-a-tat
The music stops.

Then everyone with glistening skin
Fulfilled hearts and weary limbs
Turned to go home
For when the music stops
Home is where everyone goes.

ayanwale* ayanyemi* dundun*

74   A Girl Beat Me

A fairly long time ago
Before children became men
It was one sunny day
In the crowded playing bay.

I can't recall the cause
But I remember her name
I know *Chioma* shook me up
As I fought with my tears.

I would throw a punch
But one palm to her hip
With the other palm, she would catch it
Turn it around, punching me with my own fist.

chioma*

75 THE BRAWL

Shut up!
Your words walk like a crab.

Adewale smiles
And yours stink like crap.

Adeyemi rolls his eyes, then says
You blab, my friend, you blab.

But *Adewale* laughs and replies
My friend, your words sound desperate
Desperate like a trap.

Adeyemi moves nearer him
Places his hands on his shoulder
And looks him in the eye —
I am not your friend, my friend
You run your mouth like a tap.

Adewale gets mad
And stings him with a slap
Twuaaaah!
And another slap
Twuaaaaaaaaaah!
Then raising a cloud of dust
(As the crowd throngs with cheers)

The long-coming fight begins
Within a boxing ring of limbs.

adewale* adeyemi*

76   HER BEAUTY IS

Her beauty is
The root of my smiles
An unending source of joy from within.

Her beauty is
The sun with a face
Seared with a gaze, the heat from her eyes.

Her beauty is
The shades of a glow
Hiding and seeking; the light on her skin.

Her beauty is
A pluck on a string
Tickling my ears with heavenly bliss.

Her beauty is
The dawn of a day
The dews so fresh on petals so green.

Her beauty is
The beauty of light
A spectrum of light, impinging my sight.

Her beauty is
The waves of a stream
Rising and falling like heaves of my heart.

Her beauty is
The lull of the wind
Sweetening and soothing like falling asleep.

Her beauty is the calm
Of the night
Silvery moonlight across the shoreline.

Her beauty is
The border of dreams
Intersecting with reality.

Her beauty is
The beat in my ribs
Mixed evenly with the air that I breathe.

Her beauty is
The spark in my eyes
Justifying the reason for sight.

77 A WORD ABOUT THE SUN
(FOR UDUAK)

I was curiously asked
Tell us about the sun.

So I took my time to think
And this I said after I did.

Tell me a word about those eyes
That cause a glow in other eyes
Spawning tales without a word.

Then I'll tell you about the sun
I'll tell you of Mars and Saturn
I'll tell you of planets not yet found.

uduak*

78 WELL, SO I THINK

Late for all the right things
But for the wrong ones
Always right on time
(Well, so it seems).

Maybe soon, one final haul
For once would outweigh
All that seemingly was lost
(Well, so it seems).

79 VANTAGE POINT

I'm thrown by your eyes
Far into the skies
And from this point of view
Love is beautiful.

80   OMOLOLA

Has anyone seen the evening sun from across a
beautiful distance?
A big dreamy tangerine, slowly wading home to her
cradle in the west
At those times it wears a tinge of orange and a core
of bright dancing yellow
With subtle magical glows kissing its edges all
around
Playing hide and seek with raptured clouds floating
by in fluffy obeisance
I once saw a woman blessed with such eyes — it is
perfect beauty.

Has anyone observed a dark and sleepy sky?
On those nights stars are too shy to shine
Then armies of socialising fireflies invade with
musical lights
Adorning a grateful sky and masking the trees and
bushes
With a pulsing carpet of glowing yellow snow
It is blissful beauty — like the eyes of that woman I
once saw.

I once saw (a woman with) eyes like dreamy
tangerines and glowing yellow snow
And in dutiful unison my eyes and mind had agreed
that nothing can be more beautiful
Until — the daughter of *Babaso* sashayed in with a
humble 'how-could-you' gait

And the aura of a graceful slender stem of swaying
tropical *bamboo*
(Of course un-slender in deserving places)
With eyes telling a wordless story that tie tight
invisible strings around your heart
She has beaten the record of my sight, shredding
the testimony of my eyes.

I once saw eyes like dreamy tangerines
But *Omolola's* eyes are a forest of trees
Laden with luscious fruits of dreamy tangerines
I once saw eyes like glowing yellow snow
But *Omolola's* eyes are like glowing yellow snow
But garnished with glittering purple and blue
That intersects sparkling shades of emerald and
puce.

Omolola's eyes are like a field of cockleburs
That my mind had to walk through only once
Forever ensorcelled with those kaleidoscope eyes
And the thoughts that one day, I'll sit delighted at a
table
Where her eyes are the feast and my eyes my
cutleries.

81 THE BEAUTIFUL QUESTION

The most beautiful things
In life
They say they come for free.

There is the most beautiful woman
I've ever seen
I wonder, is she free?

82 THE BEAUTIFUL ANSWER

Dusk has resumed his shift
But my brave candlelight
That I lit with my last match stick
Puts up a noble fight
Against the wind-aided night
Flickering it unsteadily
Sworn to put him out.

But it doesn't bother me
With bubbly thoughts on my mind
And a departing guest
Before my eyes.

To set myself ablaze
Is to wonder
To quell the flames
Is to ask her
Is what my mind told me.

So, on a paper patch
I wrote the beautiful question
Passed it to her and waited
She read it, smiled and scribbled
Passed it, and then took her leave.

I breathed a soft goodnight
Her words held in my hand
A smile warming my mind
But while her words
Still converged on my eyes
The nightly wind smiled in victory
As my candle lost the fight.

83   What The Paper Says

At the first streaks of dawn
I had it before my eyes
No wonder she had a smile
When a riddle was her reply.

I'm as free as dreams can be
To as many dreamers can be
With a thousand sleepless nights
Not to be endured by me.

In a race the prize is free
In a race of a thousand feet
Only a pair can pay the price
But he will not win from the stands.

84 THE GODDESS OF TIME
(FOR BLOSSOM)

Beauty like the sun, kissing the evening sea
Lands on my sight, like drunken fireflies
Opening my eyes, to a harvest of smiles
Slowly, like sand massaging sand
Sand, slowly descending an hourglass
Opening my mind, to unrefined delight
Making me pray time becomes deceased.

85 STUNNED

The gentle breeze of the waterside
Teasingly impinged my sleepy eyes
Luring me in and out of a blissful dream
Just as the morning mist cleared
Slowly, without a hurry
Un-shrouding the watery sheets
The careless wind made the ripples lap
With a gentle slap against the water bank
Leaving the shoreline pebbles whitewashed.

I stared across the river
Wiping imaginary shrouds from my eyes
As stone-stunned
Like from Medusa's spell
I was transfixed in a gaze
The mist slowly clearing
Unveiling a mannequin-perfect mystery
Slowly rising from the water like a dream
With poise slowly rising from the mist
A mystery surrounded by the mist
Somewhat like Queenly Sheba
Mounting the gold-tapered entrance
Of Solomon's byzantine court
Again and again, I rubbed my eyes
My heart loud in my ears.

All seemed to stand still —
The trees, the wind and then my breath
I looked on, looked lost
All other senses subdued by my eyes
I always thought 'beauty' was a word
Now I know it's a person —
A stranger with dark glowing skin
And jet-black hair
And dreamy eyes that cast a spell.

Slowly with careful wordless grace
This mystery scooped up some
From her liquid crystals bed
Bathing her face
As trickles raced down
Making transient art on her ebony skin.

I still stand at the shore
Watching a living dream
Then I heard a splat
On the sand, at my feet
The splat was from my lips
I did slobber like a hound
Awed by a stunner
But do I wish to be unstunned?

86   Every Woman

Every woman
In the market
Looks like you
And every girl on my bus
Wears your face
Yet I do not know you.

87 WAITING

Waiting, waitingly, waiting
Still waiting, waiting still
Waiting still, and waiting
Waiting, so waiting
As ageless time, untimely grinding slowly
Slowly slowing its ticking, teasingly
To the discomfiting creeping, of a lame sloppy snail
Heightening anxiety, exceedingly exuding gloomily
From every opening on your skin
While you are, still waiting, still
Waitingly
Waiting, yet waiting
As exasperating, unmiserly mental misery
Snippily ebbs your essence nippily
Remnant strands of patience, impatiently severed
Un-sedated, solemnly, coldly, slaying you alive
As you swear, as sure as sunrise, that time took a nap
While you keep on, waiting still
Waitingly
Waiting and waiting
Waiting with, waiting for, or waiting on?
A noble cause or on a course unjust?
Strained and dreary, drained and weary?
Or seated, sighing, blankly staring widely?
Or unsettled, pacing, perambulating wildly?
Or pretending on reading, killing time deceitfully

But time smiles, killing you instead, a tick at a time
While you yet stay, waiting still
Waitingly
Waiting, oh waiting
By careful choice or lack of one
For anything, anyone, direly or not
Like a groom, waiting on a belating flight
Dying, to embrace miles away, a waiting bride
Or like waiting, for the gratingly delaying end
Of an un-conforming and boring poem.

88 THE WALL
AND THE FORLORN

You have piled a wall around you, high
So high it blocks daylight out of my day
Wiping the faintest illusion of a smile
Away from my face.

It is no use trying to impress you
Have I not seen all those who tried?
How you wait till they reach some height
And how you shot them down with your eyes?

It is no use trying to impress you
I cannot climb over your walls
I have seen (what befell) all those who tried
I would rather crawl under it
Digging through earth
With my hand and teeth
To your feet, to find you.

And if you decide to shoot me down with your eyes
(Like you did to those who tried before)
It would not matter, I would already be down.

89   I Will Find You

My shoes
Have lost their floors
And my eyes
Riot from looking.

But till I find you
I will intently worry
Many more maps.

Till I find you
I will mercilessly scourge
Many more miles.

Till I find you
I will keenly dissect
A thousand more smiles.

I will find you.

It might take a day
Or a decade.
But I will find you.

Dust and sweat may cake my skin
But I will find you.
Hunger and thirst might rattle my bones

But I will eventually find you.
Please be waiting for me.

90 I WILL CHASE YOU NO MORE

I will chase you no more
No more, my dainty painted lady
My toes only kiss the stones
If I keep my eyes on you.

Sunlight blushes on your wings
Confessing scents like hyacinth
But you, to chase? I will no more
You're too beautiful, to be loved.

91   DARK CLOUDS

Dark clouds
Worry a beautiful sky
(But)
Dark clouds
Bring assuaging rain.

92   PURPLE DREAMER

Amidst a shore of naked thorns
I found at calm a rose un-torn
Amidst a purple dreamer's eyes
(Arrested by a single gaze)
I bathed deep in tranquil bliss.

Will my eyes, one more gaze grace?
Or would it be like yesterday
Forever buried by today
(Maybe aye, maybe nay)
Only the purple dreamer knows.

93 WHO WILL WARN IREPELOLA?

The pleasures of a journey
Of any new journey
By boat, by road or by marriage
Is it not how it tickles your imagination?

Your heart lurches in expectation
As you eagerly await the unknown
Your eyes twitch in anticipation
Of new sights soon to unfold
Your legs trip over your head
To approaching drums of adventure.

But who will warn *Irepelola?*
She has yet begun this journey
But we know she will not enjoy it
Her clothes bore imagination.

irepelola*

94   IF ONLY THEY KNEW

Heavy horse whips crack
As angry thunder in the sky
Dark shadows sprawl
Across the once peaceful sky
Joyful villagers spring out
From thirsty dusty huts
With laughter in their hands
To witness the homecoming
Of the long longed-for rain.

Little children, childish adults
They all scurry out
A procession of thirsty pots
To catch the gifts about to drop
From the sky gates flinging wide
If only they knew.

With one choral thunder blast
An impatient lightning streaked
Revealing a map of fuming clouds
Setting reins of the sky loose
Into a tantrum-throwing mood.

The pots fill up
Streets puddles form
Puddles turn to little ponds

Then the little ponds begin to turn
Into savage-looking floods
Then the smiles that marked their eyes
At the tide began to hide.

The rain had called the gales
A reign of war upon their huts
The pots lined out to catch the pour
Helplessly struggled in the flood
Roofs begin to fly like birds
Knocking real birds from the sky
Cups and dishes swim like fishes
Robes are getting washed (away)
Robbed of hope to ever hang
Once more on the owner's torso.

95   MOVING HOUSE

Memories, smiles and tears
Intangible moments amassed in the years
Swallowed up within those walls.

Those floors, a story for each spot
Toddlers' first falls, slips from misplaced toys
Hurt then anger from tacks left on the floor.

Spilled tea from dropped mugs
A tiny splinter of chinaware
You might find if you look enough.

Certain bedrooms and their corners
With memories that made wives mothers
Seeds that were sown in their sights.

Those walls bear those chalky marks
Nail bruises from framed memories
Once hanging pretty on those nails.

The entrance door and suffered knocks
Knocks, with counts like sand at sea
From every guest let in with cheers.

Laughter echoes from those walls
Family moments shared in bliss

Lost forever in timeless abyss.

Chirpy neighbours, pleasant calls
Sharing cooking recipes
Juicy gossips, masked as visits.

Each moment of victory or loss
From scrabble or monopoly wealth
Or the fall of kings to pawns.

Each window and its peculiar view
The map of your nose when pressed on it
The feel of a god — neighbours spied upon.

Meals eaten together every day
The first bite, the last bite
Tucked 'tween prayer rites.
But how can one box all these up
And pack them into a mover's truck?

96 In Memory Of Sand

I tire of these cities
Cities with concrete streets
Where have all the sand gone?
They are (now) tall buildings
Sullen, looking down on me.

I walk the streets — my feet yearn
For that beautiful sinking feel
But they are all gone
They are (now) tall buildings
Sullen, looking down on me.

97 # CHOICEST CURSE

A garment in red or a hue of blue?
A meal of grains or the fat of beef?
To turn a-right, or to the left?
Why do we ever have to choose?
Why is life not a one-page book?

98 Whatever Has No Mouth
(FOR MY LATE GRANDMA, COMFORT AKERELE)

She told her daughter on her dying bed
Write a book of me when I'm gone
Now your grandson writes a poem of you
Of how you had the face of a pretty old woman
But the springs in the feet of a teenager
Of how you taught me again and again
Failure is first a shock, then a choice —
Whatever has no mouth
Must never outsmart you.

99 THE SIGN

It was the ember tail
Of a well-spent Saturday
They sat on a bed of grass
Hers, in his hands
They spoke aloud in stares
Whispering in smiles.

Then he said —
This world always will have
Two people made of us
And when we're arm in arm
Time can never nag us
But I'm curious, it eats me
What would you do, my love
What if with some day's dawn
Without a word I'm gone
Away, not to return?

There was (true) silence and a sigh
And on her face a hint of sweat
What an imagination, my love?
But what's a world of two people
To the one who is left behind?
What a bully time would be
In a prison without walls.
Sight would double my plight

Or why would I need to see
If I won't be seeing you?
To lose my voice would be bliss
Or what comfort can be in words
If your name I cannot call?

My love, if with some day's dawn
Without a warning or a word
You are gone not to return
For several darkly nights
I will curl into a ball
To drown in tears of blood
And I won't be consoled
Then, I'll run unto the cliffs
And ask them, "Fall on me"
And if they hesitate
I'll climb upon, and jump
Your name, my dying words.

But then she beamed a smile
What an imagination we have
A bad dream — bad bad dream
That will not see daylight
Is all that can ever be
In a world that has just us
Where on us, time is no lord
Hopelessly, we are entwined
In knots that have no eye.

So they stared a little more
And smiled a little more
Then he whispered to her lips
And her hand, still in his
They rose, and walked away
Into the setting sun.

And one dawn she wore white
And some (happy) time passed
But she awoke a certain dawn
The bed still had his scent
But a hollow where he was
He was gone, he was gone
He was gone, without a word.
She knew not what to think
With hopes he'll soon return
Till high hopes became groans
As her senses laid it bare (that)
He was gone, he was gone
He was gone not to return.

For several darkly nights
She curled into a ball
She drowned in tears of blood
And could not be consoled
Then, she ran unto the cliffs
And asked them, "fall on me"
The cliffs did hesitate
So she climbed upon, and jumped

His name, her dying words.
Then she sat up, balls of sweat
Racing down her brow.

100   DEBISI

Debisi married a beast she calls her man
Her man who pounds her like a sandbag
He tans her face with heavy kicks
Smoothens her skin with slender sticks.

Shameless man
Flexing muscles on his wife
His disgrace came
When robbers came
Trading his money
For generous pummelling
Yet wife beater couldn't bite.

Wimpy man, cried like a child
That day no doubt he met his match
I swear I heard his woeful bleats
Two streets away from where I live.

If it had been poor *Debisi*
Puffing and huffing he would have
Like Matthew Murray's locomotive.

When day broke we saw his face
Swollen like a leather ball.

But it is funny what we do for love
It still was *Debisi* we saw
Gently massaging the fool
With a tender steamy sponge.

debisi*

101   Two Kisses Too Late

Time that heals all wounds with time
With time has brought me wounds.

I married a man
A man I can behold
A man that can be held
But now all I have of you
Is sound
Early when the sun yawns
The sound of your shadow
Creeping out of bed
Being careful
Not to awaken an awoken woman.

It is sound
The sound of you in the shower
Whistling under your breath
The sound of you combing your hair
Fetching your car keys
Leaving for your important job
While the janitor still snores.

It is midday
I called your office
But all I got was sound
A recorded sound of you

Asking I leave a message
So I left a message
I always do
I always have to.

Hours after the sun went to bed
The sound of you driving in
Your car headlamps dancing
On our bedroom blinds
Mocking my mind
The sound of you creeping into bed
Careful not to awaken an aching woman
The sound of you snoring all night
After a tired all day
And few hours later
The sound of your alarm clock
Handing to you the terrible baton
As the vicious cycle recycles.

I married a man
Who now doesn't know
How his house looks by day
Who has become a stranger
To the warmth of his own walls
Who walks towards the balcony
When he wants the store
Who remembers my birthday
Every other year
Who keeps forgetting

His daughter's age
Or her class in school.

I've waited, I've pleaded
I've wished things would revert
To the time we first met
Now all I have to hold
Are stale memories of old
When we ate breakfast in bed
And together shared the bath
The shadows of the times
Four o'clock was end of work
And every weekend a blessing.

I've bled in my mind
Day, noon and night
Hoping for a miracle at hand
But you were lost
Lost in your work
Lost in your thoughts
Lost in your world
You alone without us
Protecting your faults
You tell me
How you work for us
But you don't see the irony
Of how your work
Has taken you from us
You found completeness outside us.

I have bled for you
With tears like a flood
I've prayed for you
Till I lost my voice
Till it became obvious
The sound I now have
Will never again become a man
The man I loved.

Then one day
Like the sky
After the rain
The scales cleared
Off your eyes like a veil
When you lost the job
That stole you away from us
Your important job
They made you think
You alone can do.

That Tuesday in August
You trudged in torn and worn
One look, I knew all was wrong
Your eyes already convicted you
You knelt at my feet
Held my hand
Looked longingly
Into my eyes
Pleading with your eyes

You rose
Kissed my forehead
And the back of my palm.

Then memories came flooding back
When last did you hold me that way?
You told me how you still love me
How much you are sorry
But my tears flowed like a stream
When my love had turned asleep.

Already my mind was made
I had a lot on my mind
A lot to let you know
But you were never around
To hear my heart.

A lot had changed
But you were too busy to see
How I no longer called
To ask where you were
How I no more stayed awake
Each time you came back late
How I've been searching for hope
In places that are cold.

You are not the only sorry one
I've been sorry
But you never listened

You are not the only guilty one
Each day I looked so guilty
But you never noticed
You are two kisses late
For my mind is made.

102 GUILTY

Go ahead
Slap me again
If it'll ease your pain
I'll take one
For each day I've lived.

Plunge your fingers
In my eyes
Those eyes
Always searching
For what is not lost.

Slap me again
I can only stay still
Taking it humbly
Looking like I always look
Guilty!

I open my mouth
To speak but
Empty words saunter forth
What is there to say
That I've not said before?

Like the grains on a cob
I always bring home a beehive

A bear clan robbed of a cub
I wonder
Can I ever change?

103 I Wonder What He Did

I've seen him so many times
A sunken look in his sunken eyes
He exhales grief into the hills
He sits in his garden and weeps
I know he reeks with age
I know his limbs are frail
And perhaps, when his days
Still bustled with vim
He did some wrong
Now too late to set right
And all he can do
Is regret and cry.

104 # THE FALL

You stumble
You fall
(If luck smiles)
People run
To help you up
Then they are gone
Only you
Will bear the hurt.

105 PAPER BOATS AND FISHING BOATS

Sowing your seeds at noon
The sun in full bloom
It will be seven hours ago soon
When some men woke early
To till the ground and fill the heaps.
You fish in a drinking bowl
When at noon your seeds you sow.

Repose before you toil
Tomorrow assuredly spoiled
Some men all day tilled the soil
Even in rest kept sleep away
You sail in a paper boat
When you repose before you toil.

106 DAWN AND A SCARY DREAM
(FOR DAPO OSEWA)

I know this day is bowing out
I know tomorrow's dawn awaits
And I know when that dawn alights
I'll see today was merely a scary dream.

I'll find out you are at home
Trying hard to hold your laugh
At how like children we were scared
At your very thoughtless prank.

And so I'll wait until it's dawn
When this scary dream dispels.

107 A TEMPTING CONCLUSION

It is a tempting conclusion
Presented from daily hustle-bustle
But there are no bad People
Only bad people
So if you always hide indoors
From the dusty evening wind
No lovely dusk will dawn on you.

108 THE DOOR AND THE KEY

Day and night the proud door bullied his key
Men of honour daily bow under me
For a glimpse of these treasures I guard
But you — tinker scrap is what you are.

The gentle key would always humbly say
I do not compete, please let me be.

But the door will not listen
Till one day the sun was up
The key could take no more
And he got lost.

The owners searched — could not find the key
And since they had a spare, they forgot him

But more than before, day and night
The proud door heckled the spare key
Till he could take it no more
And like the one before, he got lost.

The owners searched — could not find the spare
But they had another spare.

The door harassed the other spare
More than the two that came before

Frustrated, he too got lost.

The owners searched, but could not find
And they had no more to spare
But they had another door
And they pulled the proud door down.

109 THE WORLD WE THINK WE KNOW

The days arrive
In a carriage of light
Then nights alight
Dispelling the light
Gingerly stepping
Into the husky cloak of dusk
The cycle continues
Till we no more notice it
We no more notice it
Because we're used to it.

There are people, there are issues
Agendas and motives too
Places exist, causes will never cease
But few people realise
That nothing is completely
What it is you think it is.

Won't you think it's a spade
Till a giant eats with it?
Some things, you think you know what it is
But you are a man convinced yams grow on trees
Some things, you know few things of it
But while you think that's all there is
You are that man's cousin

Who has seen birds that swim
For other things
You have no inkling it exists
(Of all, the greatest peril).

For whoever said
What you don't know won't kill you
Wasn't talking of ignorance
(No wonder he died of an unknown disease)
He wasn't talking of knowledge either
Knowledge, as deadly as ignorance
When the wisdom to put knowledge to work
Is mauled by stupid trivialising
Raped by complacency
Knowledge is dead
Till you act upon it.

I know I am ranting
But when I talk about goats
See the oats the goats swallowed
It's senseless won't mean it's insensible
It only means a little sense less
To be spotted by sensitive minds.

Politics, sociality, and economics
Just three random words?
Well maybe, maybe not.

There is a world it seems we know

Yet there is another world
Within the world we think we know
(Perhaps, it's more nested, who knows?)
Whoever said what you don't know
Won't kill you
Wasn't talking about the causes of wars
The chaos in Africa
Or the hornet's nest in the Middle East.

He wasn't talking about the food we eat
Sustaining us with slow death
Not about forces that have sworn
To illuminate our minds with darkness
He wasn't talking about modern day slavery
Television, celebrity worship or pop idols
Nor the true culprits of global warming
Nor victims of September.

He wasn't talking about mass manipulation
By the things we think make us happy
(Depends on what it is for you — music or sleep)
He wasn't talking about banks or politics
Not about the demons vying for control
From the world within the world we think we know.

110 THIS AND THAT

They say we stand aloft
Rotten venal and corrupt
They say the devil and our leaders
Are siblings of one mother
They say we feed and thrive
On deceit, greed and lies
They call us a people
Amused by self-destruction
This they say, that they say
But do they lie?

111 PAPER GLOVES

This hydra, our pain, our bane
Vicious, heinous with her steel cane
She whips us, day, noon, night the same
Disgraced, the world mocks our shame.

We've fought her over fifty years
Gallantly, our champions in *Aso Rock*
They clout, they bop, they jab, they box
From *Abuja* with their paper gloves.

Lord please help us win this fight
Earnestly we pray in our fright
Let our champions' paper punch
Crash her, quash her with a crunch.

To bring her down is all we ask
And all her harm we'll henceforth lack
We'll lock her up safely away
For we've built a jail of *papier-mâché.*

abuja* aso rock* papier-mâché*

112   HEAR (IF YOU HAVE EARS)

You make people weep, so you can live
You turn them to hopeless fools
Scorning honest men, from your fast lane
Labour — it's pride, you cruelly deride.

But nemesis lurks near at door
Soon he will crash in
He will embrace you
Like suicidal bees.

Like sudden dawn after twilight
Your shame will grow ripe
Like fatty lumps in flames
Like flames in the rain
Patiently, comeuppance awaits.

113   JONATHAN BEWARE

Jonathan beware
They might eat up wood
But termites
Dare not bite a rock.

Jonathan beware
They might knock down trees
But elephants
Dare not smash a hill.

Jonathan beware
You speak in sprinkles
To a man, un-simple in mind
He gathers the bits
With the limbs of his mind.

114 THE WAY IT IS

A mouth for greed
Will choke on it
A cute shortcut
Will cut you short.

To ride the devil's ferry
You will pay his penny
To steal from his apples
You will with him grapple.

115 MERCY WILL BE MEAN

Few true men stand
But angry bastards on the ground
Pull the few true men down
My rod spares no one
Not even one soul
Right from the sick head
To the rotten toes.

The fools who rule us
Play us for a fool
Yet the true fool is
He who lives as if
He won't die.

Voices of reason
Are drowned with more blood
Justice is not denied
For to the devils who rule
He doesn't exist.

The true fool is he
Who lives life as if
It's all about now
But a day will come
When truth will triumph
And all of these men

Who put us in a mess
Will beg for mercy
But mercy will be mean.

116   Africa Is In Me

On the shores of these seas
On the land of the southern sphere
I stand proud, Africa's stalwart
Like a sea eagle, I soar strong
Gliding above the sea's wrinkles.

I've run on the streets
An African child
Amidst rows of sun-burnt mud huts
A thin strip about my loins
I have played with loamy soil
Built domes without a scaffold.

I have fought in a thousand wars
Fearlessly, with the strength
Of a *Maasai* warrior
A heavy spear in my proud fist
My dark skin, glowing with the heat.

I have combed the tropical bush
Welcoming romantic danger
In the eyes of a leopard
I have greased the bumpy trunks
Of the mighty *Iroko* tree
With the fat of the hide
Of the leopard I skinned.

I have watched magical moonlight
Hiding and seeking on my face
I have bathed in enchanting sunset
As the end of the ageless Nile
Kisses the gold-tapered sky.

I have toiled this fruitful soil
With the edge of my heirloom plough
I have watched juicy maize shoots
Springing from my mounds
Filling my soul with hope
And I have eaten hope
From the seeds that I sowed.

Africa is in me
I'm a true-born to the skin
Would curse that day I was born
Were it on some other shore.

maasai* iroko*

117 IN BLACK AND WHITE

Fill the sea
With precious stones
Make it all mine to own
Bestow me cities
And a throne of gold
Promise me fame
With all lips on my name
But I won't trade
This skin for a day.

118 OUR FLAG WAS GREEN
(FOR NIGERIA)

Our flag was grassy green
But now it's pale like grey
By young men, stained with blood
The blood of justice cut short
By young women, stained with blood
The blood of babies unborn
The elders (pretend to) cleanse the grime
In a bowl of mud and brine.

Our flag was nobly whole
But now it's full of holes
Gaping holes on every fold
Punched in by greedy souls
No one is spared, young and the old.

Our flag was crisp
But now it stinks
Evil people piss on it
Filthy hearts seared with sin
Leary hearts without a guilt.

Our flag was green
But our hopes are heaped
That one day so close, we'll say with glee
Young, old, again, our flag is green.

119 I AM A FOOL

I am a fool
I stupidly believe
Before I have seen.

I am a fool
I have faith in a big book
By men who knew no school.

I am a fool
I believe iron floats
And animals can speak.

I am a fool
I believe the skies rained flames
And the sun stood still.

I am a fool
I believe screams and songs
Made a thick wall fall.

I am a fool
I believe water turned wine
And two fishes made a feast.

I am a fool
I believe rods eat snakes

And words raise the dead.

I am a fool
But I know another fool
Who says there is no God.

120 The Deviant's Anthem

I wait
But not like one who waits
I wait, like at the end
From the beginning.

I hope
Not like I'm left to fate
I hope like tomorrow
When with the sun comes dawn.

I trust
Not like without a choice
I trust, like it's my choice
In a WORD that cannot fail.

121 A REPOSE SUPPLICATION

The scythed sister of sleep
Lurks grimly, close to her sib'
Seeking company across the sea
A thin line, between death and sleep
To sorrowful pleas or unending bliss.

Gracious Lord watch over me
Each time I lay to slumber in peace
Let angelic wings cover me
Each time I make my dreamy trip
So I don't slip off in my sleep.

122 THE VISITOR

You may know where I live
But my home
Is none of these busy cities
Home is beyond the hills
Behind gates of pearls
Upon streets of gold.

123 ## ONE, TWO, THREE
(FOR MY FATHER)

Like one, two, three
This is a simple one
When I know better
Than to try saying
Simple things complicatedly —
Dad, I love you.

INTERESTING WORDS

Abuja [ah-boo-jah]
>   The capital city of Nigeria, West Africa, which is also where the Nigerian Presidential complex is situated.

Agbada [ah-gba-dah]
>   An important and sometimes ceremonial flowing gown, typically large and worn by men in West Africa, especially by the Yoruba people (Nigeria). It often signifies the wearer is wealthy or influential.

Ayomide [ah-yaw-mi-deh]
>   A usually male given name of Yoruba, Nigeria origin. It literally means "my joy has come".

Amala [ah-mah-lah]
>   A Yoruba, (Nigeria) meal made from peeled yam, dried and blended into flour. It is served as a thick brown paste and often eaten with soup.

Ayan-wale, Ayan-yemi [ah-yuhn-wah-leh] [ah-yuhn-yeh-mi]
>   These Yoruba (Nigeria) names are derived from the family vocation of the bearers. *Ayan* means drummer. *Ayan-wale* literally means the 'drummer

has come home' and *Ayanyemi;* 'I am fit to be a drummer'.

Ade-wale, Ade-yemi [ah-deh-wah-leh] [ah-deh-yeh-mi]
Ade means 'crown' (Yoruba language, Nigeria), and the name often infers royalty. *Ade-wale* means 'the crown has come home' or 'royalty has come home'. *Adeyemi* means 'I am worthy of the crown' or 'I am worthy of royalty'.

Aso Rock [ah-soh rok]
Nigerian Presidential villa, named after a large and prominent outcrop on the outskirts of Abuja, Nigeria's capital city.

Bamboo [bam-boo]
A thin tree-like tropical grass.

Baobab [bah-oh-bab]
A native tropical African tree with an exceedingly large trunk.

Chi-oma [chi-haw-mah]
Igbo language, Nigeria. Literally translates to 'good god', but more accurately means 'you have a good god' as it is believed everyone has a personal 'god' or '*chi*' that guides them'. People who have a bad '*chi*' or 'god' are people who often experience misfortune or

calamity in life, while people with a good *'chi'* or 'god' rarely encounter misfortuns. The name is hence a way of wishing a baby good luck in life.

'Debisi [deh-bee-see]

A contracted form of the name *Adebisi*. A given Yoruba name (mostly female) which literally means 'the crown has increased'. *Ade* literally means 'crown'. It is often associated with royal families. *Adebisi* hence could mean 'the royal family has increased' (with the birth of the new baby).

Dolapo [daw-lah-kpo]

A usually female Yoruba (Nigeria) given name, a contracted form of *Oluwadolapo*, which literally means 'God has added wealth unto wealth' as the new child is seen as from God, and a welcome increase or wealth to the family.

Dun-dun [doon-doon]

Also called the 'talking drum'. It is a cultural and entertainment double-headed drum of the Yoruba people of Nigeria, whose pitch can be controlled to mimic the rhythm, stress and intonation of human speech.

Fufu [foo-foo]

A dough-like West African meal made from boiled cassava and eaten with stew.

Gbegiri [gbe-gi-ri]

A West African bean soup, popular among the Yoruba people of Nigeria.

Irepelola [i-re-kpe-law-lah]

Yoruba Language (Nigeria). While it is not a real word or given name, *Irepelola* is made up of two real Yoruba words; *Irepe* which mean 'a strip of' (as of clothing) and *Ola* which means 'Dignity' or 'Splendour'. *Irepelola* however does not translate to 'a strip of dignity or splendour', — instead it connotes 'one who finds dignity in strips' (as against decent clothing).

Iroko [i-roh-koh]

A large tropical hardwood tree of West Africa.

Iya Bose [i-ya boh-seh]

Yoruba language, Nigeria. It is common in many African cultures for friends and neighbours to refer to parents by the names of their children, (usually the first child's). *Iya Bose* means 'Bose's Mother'. *Bose* means 'the one who came with a new week' or 'the one who came on a Sunday'. (Although the day of the week is not referred to in the phrase, Sunday is often considered as the beginning of a new week, especially in Yoruba culture).

Juju [joo-joo]
A form of West African magic.

Maasai [muh-sahy]
A nomadic people near Kenya who had fearsome reputations as warriors and cattle thieves.

Mamihlapinatapai [ma-mi-la-pi-na-ta-pa-e]
Yaghan language of Tierra del Fuego. A word describing the look two people share which expresses a mutual desire which neither of them is willing to be the first to verbally confirm. It has been described by the Guinness World Records as the most succinct word in the world.

Oga [aw-gah]
Yoruba language, Nigeria. Means 'Boss' or 'Leader'.

Oleku [oh-le-koo]
Yoruba language, Nigeria. Used to describe something or someone that is outstanding.

Olufunmi [oh-loo-foon-mi]
Yoruba language, Nigeria. A contracted form of the female name *Oluwafunmi* which means 'God has

given me...' The name often ends with what has been given e.g. *Oluwafunmilola* means 'God has given me wealth' and 'Oluwafunmilayo' means 'God has given me joy'.

Painted Lady [peyn-tid, ley-dee]
   A type of colourful butterfly.

Papier-mâché [pey-per-muh-shey]
   An art object made entirely from paper strips soaked in starch paste for a binder.

Sawubona [sa-woo-boh-nah]
   A South African greeting that literally means 'I see you'. It is a deeply insightful way of acknowledging the other person's existence. It is like saying I appreciate you, I recognise you as important, and it buttresses the truth that people are people because of other people.

Tosin [toh-seen]
   Yoruba language, Nigeria. A male or female given name which is a contracted from of *Oluwatosin*. It means, 'The Lord is worthy to be worshipped'.

Uduak [ooh-doo-ak]

Ibiobio language, Nigeria. A usually female given name which means 'God's Wish' or 'God's will'.

Uju [ooh-joo]

Igbo language, Nigeria. *Uju* is a shortened form of *Obianuju*. It is a female given name which literally means 'born into wealth'.

Wahala [wah-ah-lah]

Nigerian pidgin word of Hausa origin. It means 'trouble' or 'bother'.

Dear reader,

Thank you for getting a copy of this book. I really hope you enjoyed reading the poems. If you did, please leave a review on any of the online bookstores.

Thank you and God bless.

Tolu' Akinyemi

Tolu', leaning on one of the four gigantic fluted columns guarding the massive Greek Doric entrance portico on the west end of St Matthew's Anglican Church Brixton. The building, designed by Charles Ferdinand Porden (1790-1863) is a grade II 'listed building' (on the Statutory List of Buildings of Special Architectural or Historic Interest in the UK) since 1951. The foundation stone was laid in 1824 and it was consecrated two years later. Insert taken circa 1912. (Source, Lambeth Archives).

Printed in Great Britain
by Amazon.co.uk, Ltd.,
Marston Gate.